CONSTELLATION CHART

NORTHERN HEMISPHERE

PISCES
EQUULEUS
PEGASUS
ANDROMEDA
ARIES
CETUS
DELPHINUS
TRIANGULUM
SAGITTA
LACERTA
PERSEUS
TAURUS
CYGNUS
VULPECULA
CASSIOPEIA
CEPHEUS
AQUILA
LYRA
ORION
DRACO
URSA MINOR
AURIGA
CAMELOPARDALIS
GEMINI
HERCULES
LYNX
CANIS MINOR
OPHIUCHUS
CANCER
CORONA BOREALIS
LEO MINOR
SERPENS
HYDRA
CANES VENATICI
BOÖTES
URSA MAJOR
COMA BERENICES
LEO
VIRGO

D0319949

SECRETS IN THE SKIES

Giles Sparrow
James Weston Lewis

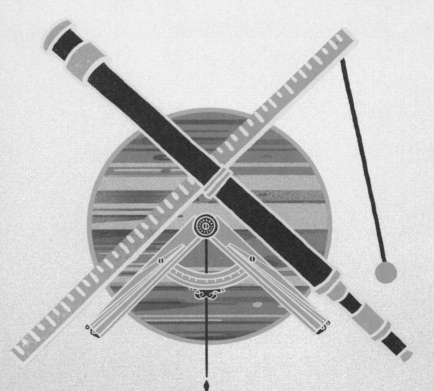

wren
&rook

'In questions of science, the authority of a thousand is not worth the humble reasoning of a single individual.'

Galileo Galilei

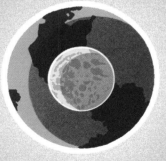

CONTENTS

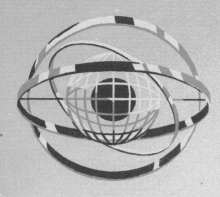

DANGEROUS FALL

One bright and sunny morning around 1590, or so the story goes, a curious crowd gathered beneath the Leaning Tower of Pisa in northern Italy. Standing at the very top of the tower was Galileo Galilei, the rebellious professor of mathematics at the local university. He held two balls in his hands, identical in size but each a different weight.

The murmuring crowd watched as he released the balls and they plummeted through the air. Everyone knew they would fall at different speeds depending on their weight – the famous scholar Aristotle, who had gone unquestioned for 2,000 years, had said so. And yet …

THUD!

The two balls struck the ground at exactly the same moment. When they did, Galileo's revolutionary theory, that Earth's gravity affects all objects in the same way regardless of their weight, was proved right. Aristotle's ideas had been dealt a fatal blow, paving the way for a scientific revolution.

Today's experts think the tale of Galileo's Leaning Tower experiment is just that – a story invented long after his death. But why do people still repeat myths about him centuries later? Perhaps it's because Galileo attracted plenty of drama in his own lifetime – he sparked a revolution, confronted powerful authorities and risked his life.

But in truth, Galileo's story started much earlier than the sixteenth century – after all, humankind has always been fascinated by the secrets in the skies …

SECRETS IN THE SKIES

Our prehistoric ancestors stared at the stars and saw patterns, inspiring them to tell stories and create cave-wall paintings that still survive today.

We call these patterns constellations and we can spot them just as our ancestors did. The sky doesn't stay still, though. Rising in the east and setting in the west, the Sun, Moon and stars appear to move across it each day.

Scorpius

Taurus

Leo

Orion

Early stargazers couldn't tell the Earth was moving, so they concluded that the heavens were fixed to a spinning 'celestial sphere', with Earth sitting still at its centre.

But later night-time observers knew it couldn't be that simple, as not every object in the sky moved in the same way. The Moon changed its shape and moved through the constellations each night, while the Sun took a year to move through a band of constellations called the zodiac. Other objects looked like bright stars but moved around the zodiac on complicated, looping paths. Astronomers in ancient Greece called these puzzling objects 'planets', from a word for 'wanderer'.

Untangling these curious movements took thousands of years, but it was the key to understanding our true place in the universe.

NERGAL
OR
MARS

MARDUK
OR
JUPITER

ISHTAR
OR
VENUS

The earliest astronomers were also astrologers – they believed that celestial objects influenced lives on Earth.

Because of their supposed power, the planets were linked with gods. Stargazers in the ancient Middle Eastern region of Mesopotamia named the brightest planets after Nergal, the god of war; Marduk, the king of the gods; and Ishtar, the goddess of beauty. Astronomers in Rome kept these ideas, but named the planets after their own gods: Nergal became Mars, Marduk became Jupiter and Ishtar became Venus.

Most people didn't believe the planets *were* gods, but many thought that their movements could indicate what the gods were up to. For example, if a king died violently in battle when Nergal and Marduk passed close to each other in the sky, the king's successor might well think twice about starting a new war when the two planets next encountered each other.

So predicting the movements of the planets became hugely important, but pinning them down proved tricky. Instead of following straight-line tracks in the sky, they often made strange, mysterious loops that were hard to explain. Mercury and Venus always stayed close to the Sun, while Mars, Jupiter and Saturn circled the entire sky. What was the answer to this puzzle?

The ancient Greeks took a very different approach to understanding the universe. Thinkers, called philosophers, believed that the planets and stars moved according to rules of nature that hadn't been discovered yet.

Many philosophers thought the best way of discovering these rules was through debate – imagining each possible way the universe might work, then arguing about which one was best. But one scholar took a different approach ...

Aristotle lived in the fourth century BCE and studied everything from ethics to botany and zoology. Before he turned his attention to the solar system, he even tutored Alexander the Great! What set Aristotle apart was that he believed in studying the real world, then coming up with theories fitting what he observed. He's often described as the first true scientist.

Aristotle imagined Earth as a perfect ball at the centre of the universe, surrounded by several hollow, transparent spheres each spinning steadily. Think of it like an onion, which has a central core surrounded by many layers. The Moon sat on the sphere closest to Earth. Then came Mercury, Venus, the Sun, Mars, Jupiter, Saturn, and a final outer sphere of stars. Aristotle's idea was simple, elegant – and wrong.

Although Aristotle had a huge influence, it didn't take long for stargazers to realise that his ideas didn't predict the planets' movements very well. His theory needed fixing.

Claudius Ptolemy lived in Alexandria, on the north coast of Egypt, in the second century. Alexandria was a melting pot – originally founded by Aristotle's student Alexander the Great, by Ptolemy's time it was a key city in the Roman Empire. People came from far and wide to study at Alexandria's great library, home to knowledge from around the world.

Ptolemy distilled all this wisdom into books. His masterwork, the *Almagest*, listed the constellations and offered a new explanation for the movement of the planets. Onto Aristotle's spheres, Ptolemy attached smaller spinning tracks. Each planet moved on its track, as well as being carried around by Aristotle's larger spheres. Ptolemy's theory helped explain why a planet sometimes seemed to reverse across the sky.

Ptolemy's ideas spread like wildfire – they were studied in India, Persia, the Islamic world and medieval Europe. But there was trouble brewing ...

GODLY THINKING

The Roman Empire dominated Europe and the Near East for hundreds of years, spreading the ideas of scholars such as Aristotle and Ptolemy, but it collapsed during the fifth century. Ancient science was lost to Western Europe, but the Roman Catholic church remained powerful.

Ptolemy and Aristotle's ideas seemed to back up the Bible's story of creation. For example, the Bible suggests God created the Earth first, then made the Sun and Moon as lights to rule day and night. It also describes the Sun moving through the sky. Questioning the Bible was dangerous – it could get you expelled from the Church, or even killed.

But elsewhere, things were different. As the religion of Islam spread through the Middle East from 634 CE, Islamic scholars eagerly collected writings from Greece, Rome and beyond, and tried to improve on them.

Islamic astronomy flourished. New instruments for measuring the positions of stars and planets were invented, such as the astrolabe perfected by Mariam 'Al-Astrolabiya' Al-Ijliya. These measurements challenged Ptolemy's system and, over centuries, this questioning approach began to filter back into Europe. It was the start of the Renaissance, when art and science bloomed.

CHANGE IN THE HEAVENS

Around 1450, word began to spread of a remarkable new invention –
a German man named Johannes Gutenberg had made a machine that
could print books quickly and cheaply. Ideas could travel much more
widely and rapidly than ever before.

Printed summaries of Ptolemy's *Almagest* soon appeared and, around
1496, one fell into the hands of a young Polish priest. Nicolaus Copernicus
became fascinated by Ptolemy's ideas, but when he looked at the stars
and planets for himself, he discovered that they often didn't move as
he expected.

In 1514, Copernicus wrote a book that he sent to some trusted friends. In it, he showed how the planets' movements could be explained if the Sun was at the centre of the universe, with the Earth being one of six planets circling around it. Venus and Mercury were closer to the Sun than Earth, which was why they never moved far from the Sun in the sky. Mars, Jupiter and Saturn were further out, appearing to move backwards when the faster-moving Earth overtook them.

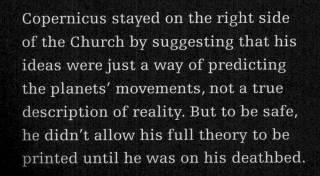

Copernicus stayed on the right side of the Church by suggesting that his ideas were just a way of predicting the planets' movements, not a true description of reality. But to be safe, he didn't allow his full theory to be printed until he was on his deathbed.

THE BOY FROM PISA

In November 1572, people across Europe stared up in fear and wonder at a strange new sight in the night sky. A brilliant new star had appeared in the constellation of Cassiopeia, outshining everything except the Moon. What did it mean? Dukes and queens hurried to consult their court astrologers, while people on the streets murmured about the end of the world.

In the northern Italian town of Pisa, an eight-year-old boy named Galileo Galilei probably gazed out from his bedroom at the new star shining over the city's huddled rooftops. It would have been unlike this curious boy to miss out on something so exciting.

Galileo was living with a merchant called Muzio Tedaldi – his parents Vincenzo and Giulia had moved to Florence earlier in the year.

The young boy filled his days making models and miniature machines – he loved investigating the world around him. Muzio wasn't that surprised – Galileo's father Vincenzo was a famous lute player and was very curious too. He had made a name for himself by testing theories about music, often proving the theories wrong.

THE INVENTIVE GENIUS

In 1581, the 17-year-old Galileo joined the University of Pisa. Vincenzo hoped his son might become a doctor.

But Galileo's mind often wandered. One day, sitting in the quiet vastness of Pisa Cathedral, he noticed a lamp laden with sweet-smelling incense, swaying back and forth in a perfect rhythm.

Fascinated, he soon worked out that the rhythm of a swinging weight, called a pendulum, depends only on the length of string supporting it. He then invented a device that used a pendulum to measure a person's pulse rate.

Galileo had found his calling, and asked his father to pay for him to have a tutor in maths. He learned fast, and by the age of 25 he was made a professor.

Before long Galileo moved to a better-paid job at the University of Padua. He earned extra money by inventing new machines and measuring devices that he could make and sell.

Water pump
Powered by a horse, could draw water from below ground to irrigate fields.

Hydrostatic balance
Allowed jewellers to work out the mixture of gold and silver in an object.

Thermoscope
Showed how hot or cold it was by the height of a column of water.

Military compass
Accurately measured the firing angle and range of cannons.

THE TELESCOPE

By 1609, Galileo was 45 years old and troubled by nagging health problems. Work at Padua was still not bringing in enough money, as Galileo's commitments now included a partner and three young children.

But that year, he got word of an amazing discovery from the Netherlands. A Dutch spectacle-maker, Hans Lippershey, had found that if he put curved glass lenses at each end of a simple tube, he could make an image that was magnified much more than a single lens alone could manage.

Eyepiece

The eyepiece lens made the object seem much closer because it spread out the light entering the telescope across the retina of the eye.

Galileo set out to build his own version of this new device, called the telescope. His experience with inventing helped, and soon he was making much better telescopes than anyone else.

Objective Lens

The telescope's first, larger lens, called the objective, bent rays of light from distant objects on to paths that drew closer together inside the telescope.

Galileo's first telescope made distant objects appear three times larger than they did with an unaided eye. Just a year later, he had improved this to a magnification of 30 times.

THE FAR-SEEING EYE

Galileo hadn't forgotten his time with his father's merchant friend Muzio, and realised that his new device could be the answer to his money worries. In August 1609, he took his much-improved telescope to Venice. The city was wealthy and powerful thanks to its shipping trade, but lived in fear of attacks from the Turkish navy. Galileo knew the city's officials would be interested in his offer.

One fine morning, he invited city leaders to the top of the mighty Saint Mark bell tower in the heart of Venice. There, he revealed a telescope that could magnify objects by eight times, letting city leaders spot both merchant vessels and raiders that were still well out at sea, giving them time to make preparations or defend an attack.

The Venetians immediately saw the potential – they doubled Galileo's Padua salary, and paid handsomely for the telescope itself.

THE STARRY MESSENGER

From late 1609, Galileo turned his telescope to the sky. He had been dabbling in astronomy since 1604, when another brilliant new star, or 'nova', similar to the one that appeared in his childhood, had erupted in the sky. Galileo had given lectures on the nova, and had shown that it must be immensely far away from Earth.

Aristotle, Ptolemy and the Catholic Church all said that the heavens beyond the Moon were a perfect creation of God and could never change, but Galileo's studies of the nova said different. And when he looked through the telescope he found even more signs of change …

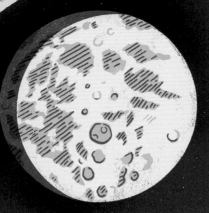

The Moon had an uneven surface including deep craters and towering mountains that cast shadows.

Each constellation was filled with faint stars, and the pale band of the Milky Way was made of star clouds.

Jupiter was a disc, not a point of light, and had four moons of its own that danced around it.

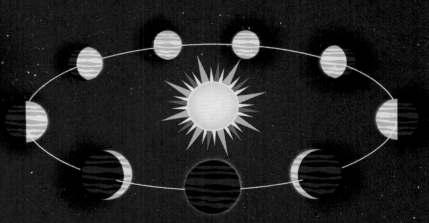

Saturn had strange bumps on each side (his telescope wasn't powerful enough to reveal that these were actually rings).

Venus looked like a small disc sometimes, and like a much larger crescent at others.

Galileo wrote about some of these discoveries in a book called *The Starry Messenger*. People doubted his claims at first, but as other telescopes improved, they became undeniable. Galileo's work turned him into a celebrity.

ALLIES AND ENEMIES

Galileo's discoveries convinced him that the Copernican theory of a universe with the Sun at its centre had to be right. The moons of Jupiter proved that not everything revolved around Earth, and the changing shape of Venus made sense only if Venus orbited the Sun. This led Galileo into dangerous territory – influential scholars, called Jesuits, had built their reputations on Aristotle's ideas.

Galileo returned to Pisa to become court philosopher to the grand duke of Tuscany. At first, things seemed to go well. Galileo took his telescope to Rome and impressed Jesuit leaders, and made allies such as nobleman Federico Cesi and writer Margherita Sarrocchi.

But as Galileo began to write more widely, he soon overstepped the mark. In 1613, he published letters describing his discovery of dark spots on the Sun. In them, he made the mistake of outlining how his work supported the ideas of Copernicus.

AGAINST THE INQUISITION

Religious scholars began to attack Galileo's views. Most Catholics of the time believed that the words of the Bible were literally true, so there was a lot of argument about the precise meaning of each and every sentence.

In 1615, Galileo wrote a letter to Tuscany's grand duchess explaining how Bible passages suggesting the Sun moved could be matched up with Copernican theory. Religious scholars were outraged – how dare a mathematician claim to understand the Bible better than they did?

Galileo was called to Rome for a trial before the religious court, the Inquisition. The stakes were huge – heresy could get you executed. Fortunately, Galileo had powerful friends in parts of the Church, and some other scholars agreed with him that the Bible and this newly discovered scientific knowledge did not necessarily contradict each other.

The trial ended with a compromise. Galileo was given a stern telling-off and ordered not to teach the Sun-centred universe as the truth – but he could continue discussing it as a way to predict the movements of the planets.

NOT MY SOLAR SYSTEM

HELIO-CENTRISM IS RUBBISH

GAL-I-LAME-O

THE DANGEROUS *DIALOGUE*

For the next few years, Galileo steered clear of astronomy, but he couldn't avoid getting into arguments. In 1623, he wrote a book setting out his approach of using experimentation and maths to understand the world. Its attacks on his rivals set Jesuit scholars even more fiercely against him. Fortunately the new pope, Urban VIII, was a supporter of Galileo.

The pope gave the book his seal of approval, and when Galileo visited, he encouraged him to write more about the nature of the universe. Inspired, Galileo began work on a book he called the *Dialogue Concerning the Two Chief World Systems*.

In it, he imagined rival Copernican and Aristotelian philosophers trying to convince a third person that their theory was best. He avoided arguing that the Copernican view was true, but he couldn't resist making the Aristotelian philosopher look foolish.

When the *Dialogue* was published in 1632, Galileo discovered he had offended many of his powerful friends, including the pope. The Inquisition threatened to drag Galileo to Rome in chains if he did not come willingly to explain himself ...

THE TRIAL

In early 1633, 69-year-old Galileo found himself on trial once more. Through five months of questioning and under threat of torture, the frail, fierce man denied saying that Copernicanism was true.

He was fighting a losing battle – the way the *Dialogue* was written made his true position obvious, and Galileo was forced to admit that the book could be seen as favouring a Sun-centred universe.

Galileo was sentenced to life imprisonment, though this became house arrest. The *Dialogue* was banned across Catholic Europe, along with anything he might write in future. Worst of all, he was forced to publicly deny the idea that Earth moved around the Sun.

Did Galileo give up his beliefs in the end? No one knows for sure, but a legend soon arose that after giving a final, fateful speech in court, he muttered softly under his breath: 'and yet, it moves!'

AND YET, IT MOVES!

In 1633, Galileo returned home to his hillside villa outside Florence where he would remain for the rest of his life. He spent his final years lost in work, and in 1638 printed his last book, *Discourse on Two New Sciences*. It had to be smuggled to Holland to be printed, but it had a huge influence – Galileo set out proof for the 'law of falling bodies' he had first investigated all those years ago at Pisa, and laid the foundations for the science of gravity.

That same year, Galileo went blind –
he would never see the stars again. But still
he kept busy, welcoming visitors, debating new
discoveries and even inventing a pendulum clock that
was decades ahead of its time.

Galileo died in January 1642, aged 77. The grand
duke planned to bury him with honour in Florence's
magnificent Santa Croce Church, but the pope
intervened – burying a convicted heretic in such a
prominent place was out of the question. Instead,
Galileo was laid to rest in a nearby chapel.

SEEING PAST THE STORIES

Today, Galileo is seen as a hero of science. His fearless support for evidence against accepted wisdom, and his methods of measurement and mathematics, put him at the forefront of the scientific revolution that shaped our modern world. The fight with Galileo fatally undermined the Church's claim to be the final authority on the nature of the universe, freeing science to follow its own path.

In 1737, Galileo was reburied in the main Santa Croce church. A century of discovery had proved his ideas essentially right – even if the real solar system turned out to be more complex than he had imagined.

During the reburial ceremony, priests removed relics from Galileo's body. A magnificent monument depicted him gazing at the sky, a telescope in one hand and a book in the other, flanked by figures of astronomy and geometry. He was treated more like a saint than a heretic.

Yet the Church was still slow to admit its mistake and lift the bans on Galileo's books. It was not until 1992, more than 400 years later, that Pope John Paul II issued a formal apology for Galileo's persecution.

IN GALILEO'S FOOTSTEPS

Galileo first looked through a telescope more than four centuries ago. Since then, generations of scientists have discovered a universe more complex than he could ever have imagined.

BENJAMIN BANNEKER
He calculated the paths of the Sun, Moon and planets with great precision, publishing them in almanacs from 1792.

FRIEDRICH BESSEL
In 1838, he used Earth's motion around the Sun to show that other stars were many light years (millions of millions of kilometres) from Earth.

WILLIAM AND CAROLINE HERSCHEL
In 1784–5, these sibling astronomers mapped the pattern of stars in the sky and worked out the rough shape of our Milky Way galaxy.

JAMES BRADLEY
Around 1725, he discovered that the angle of starlight reaching Earth changes throughout the year – proof that we orbit around the Sun.

ISAAC NEWTON
In 1687, he expanded Galileo's ideas about the motion of objects, and explained the orbits of planets and moons through the force of gravity.

ANNIE JUMP CANNON

In the early twentieth century, she measured starlight in ways that helped reveal the size, temperature and brightness of distant suns.

STEPHEN HAWKING

Born almost 300 years after Galileo died, he investigated gravity, and the beginning and end of the universe.

ALBERT EINSTEIN

His famous theories of relativity, explaining the true nature of gravity and space, developed from Galileo's fundamental principles.

VERA RUBIN

In the 1970s, she showed that galaxies contain vast amounts of invisible dark matter – a mysterious substance that outweighs normal matter by six to one!

HENRIETTA SWAN LEAVITT

In 1912, she discovered a way of finding the true brightness of stars over great distances – the key to measuring the larger universe.

KATHERINE JOHNSON

In the 1950s and 1960s, she used the laws of gravity to calculate flight paths and orbits around the Earth for the first US astronauts.

EDWIN HUBBLE

In the 1920s, he used Leavitt's discovery to show that other galaxies are millions of light years beyond the Milky Way, and that the universe is expanding at tremendous speed.

GEORGES LEMAÎTRE

In 1927, this Catholic priest proposed that the universe was born in a huge explosion in the distant past: the Big Bang.

TOUCHING THE STARS

The telescopes Galileo used to look at the heavens were just the start of the story. Today, astronomers use instruments much bigger than he could ever have imagined to sweep up light from the stars and uncover their secrets.

While Galileo's telescope used lenses, most of today's giants use huge curved mirrors to gather up light and direct it to cameras and other devices that can study it. The biggest telescope in the world, currently being built in Chile, has a main mirror measuring 39.3 m across – bigger than a tennis court. It gathers up 10 million times more light than the human eye.

Today, human flights to space stations in orbit around the Earth are commonplace. We've even put robot telescopes such as the Hubble Space Telescope into space, where they can see more clearly into the distant depths of the universe.

A space probe named after
Galileo orbited Jupiter for
eight years. The images it
sent back transformed our
understanding of the giant
planet and the four huge
moons that Galileo himself
discovered.

Our robot spacecraft have travelled to the planets
and moons Galileo saw through his telescope,
sending back stunning photographs. And now,
some of these robot probes are even on their way
beyond the solar system, carrying messages from
humanity towards distant stars.

HOW THE SOLAR SYSTEM REALLY WORKS

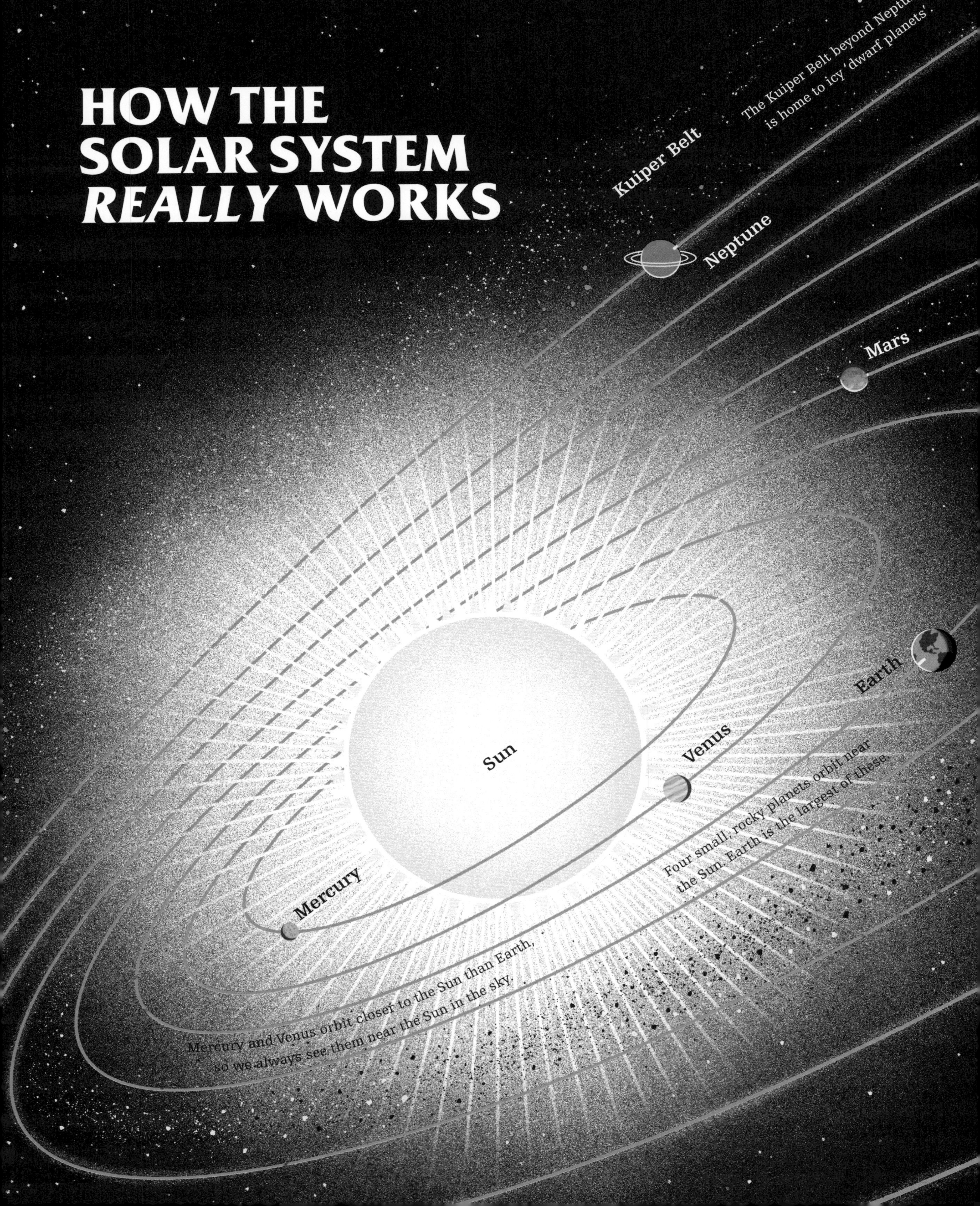

The Kuiper Belt beyond Neptune is home to icy 'dwarf planets'

Kuiper Belt

Neptune

Mars

Sun

Venus

Earth

Mercury

Four small, rocky planets orbit near the Sun. Earth is the largest of these.

Mercury and Venus orbit closer to the Sun than Earth, so we always see them near the Sun in the sky.

Saturn

The asteroid belt contains many thousands of small, rocky worlds orbiting between Mars and Jupiter.

Orbits are not perfect circles, but stretched circles called ellipses.

Four much bigger planets made of gas and liquid orbit further out. Jupiter is the biggest of all.

Uranus

Asteroid belt

Jupiter

Planets move faster when they are closer to the Sun and more slowly when they are further away.

Comets are small icy objects in stretched orbits. When they come close to the Sun, they heat up and can develop spectacular tails.

comet

45

GLOSSARY

Astrolabe
A disc-shaped measuring device that allows astronomers to accurately measure angles in the sky, and predict the rising and setting times of different objects.

Astrology
The belief that the movement of celestial objects either influences or reflects events on Earth.

Astronomy
The science of measuring and understanding stars, planets and other objects in space.

Big Bang
The huge explosion that most scientists think created the universe 13.8 billion years ago.

Celestial
A word describing any object in the sky.

Constellation
A pattern made out of bright stars in the night sky, invented by humans.

Contradiction
When two pieces of knowledge or writing say things that are the opposite of each other, so they cannot both be correct.

Copernicanism
The idea that the Earth is just one of many planets orbiting around the Sun, promoted by Nicolaus Copernicus.

Crater
A bowl-shaped dent in the surface of a planet or moon, usually made when the celestial object is hit at high speed by a rock from space.

Galaxy
A huge cloud of stars, planets, gas, dust and other objects held together by gravity. Galaxies have many different shapes, but a lot of them are spirals.

Gravity
A force that pulls things towards very large objects such as planets and stars.

Heliocentrism
The idea that the Sun is at the centre of the solar system.

Heretic
Someone who does not believe in the teachings of a particular religion.

Inquisition
A religious court created by the Roman Catholic Church to investigate heretics.

Islam
A religion founded by the prophet Mohammed in the early 600s, which spread rapidly across the Middle East, North Africa and eventually into southern Europe.

Jesuit
A branch of the Christian Church founded in 1534 to defend Catholic beliefs.

Lens
A piece of curved glass that bends the path of light rays passing through it.

Light
A type of energy produced by certain objects, which our eyes can see and use to interpret the world around us. Stars (including the Sun) release light that spreads out in rays and reflects off many other objects, allowing us to see them.

Lute
A musical instrument with a long 'neck', strings and a round body.

Magnify
To make something appear larger than it would to an unaided human eye.

Matter
The stuff that makes up all the objects in the universe.

Medieval
A period of history in Europe (from around 500 to 1500) when most countries were ruled by kings and queens, the Christian Church was very powerful, and ancient writings were treated as the most important source of knowledge.

Milky Way
The galaxy that contains our solar system. The Milky Way is a flattened spiral, and because we sit inside it, we see most of its stars as a band of light across the sky.

Nova
A bright 'new' star in the sky, caused by a distant, faint star undergoing a violent explosion.

Orbit
The path one object (such as a planet) takes around another one (such as the Sun) under the control of gravity.

Pendulum
A weight that swings back and forth on the end of a rod, chain or string.

Persecution
Bullying or threatening someone, often because of political or religious difference.

Planet
A large ball of rock or gas that orbits around a star, and may have moons and rings orbiting around it in turn.

Pope
The head of the Roman Catholic Church.

Pulse rate
The rate at which blood pumps around your body, driven by your heartbeat.

Relic
An object (such as a piece of clothing) from a highly respected person (such as a Christian saint) kept after their death to help people to remember their importance.

Renaissance
A period of history (roughly from the late 1300s to the 1600s) when scholars and artists in Europe experimented with new ideas and methods.

Roman Catholic Church
A branch of the Christian Church that was particularly powerful in Europe from the end of the Roman Empire through to medieval times. In Galileo's lifetime, its dominance was being challenged by the rise of a rival form of Christianity called Protestantism.

Roman Empire
A network of countries across Europe, Asia and north Africa that was ruled by emperors in Rome between 27 BCE and 476 CE.

Solar system
The region of space dominated by the Sun's gravity, and all the objects that lie within it, following orbits around the Sun.

Star
A huge ball of gas that glows hot enough to generate light, and which has enough gravity to hold planets and other objects in orbit around it.

Telescope
A device that uses lenses or mirrors to capture light rays from distant objects and create a brighter, magnified image.

Theory
An idea about what might cause something to happen. Scientists test theories to see how well they match reality – when they fail, then the theory must be improved or replaced.

Weight
A force created by gravity pulling on an object with a property called mass (which includes most types of matter).

Zodiac
A band of constellations wrapped around the sky, where the Sun and planets are usually seen.

First published in Great Britain in 2019 by Wren & Rook

ISBN: 978 1 5263 6001 4
E-book ISBN: 978 1 5263 6183 7
10 9 8 7 6 5 4 3 2 1

MIX
Paper from
responsible sources
FSC® C104740

FSC
www.fsc.org

Wren & Rook
An imprint of
Hachette Children's Group
Part of Hodder & Stoughton
Carmelite House
50 Victoria Embankment
London EC4Y 0DZ

An Hachette UK Company
www.hachette.co.uk
www.hachettechildrens.co.uk

Publishing Director: Debbie Foy
Senior Editor: Liza Miller
Art Director: Laura Hambleton

Printed in China